LETT

Five Meditations ... ...tual Journey
with Prayers, Poems and Drawings
from Maypole Farm

LETTING GO

Five Meditations on the Spiritual Journey
with Prayers, Poems and Drawings
from Maypole Farm

by

William C. Denning

John Hunt
Publishing Limited

Copyright © 2001 John Hunt Publishing Ltd
Text and illustrations © William C. Denning 2001

ISBN 1 84298-004-1

Designed by Graham Whiteman Design

All rights reserved. Except for brief quotations in critical articles or reviews, no part of this book may be reproduced in any manner without prior written permission from the publishers.

Write to:
John Hunt Publishing Ltd
46A West Street
Alresford
Hampshire SO24 9AU
UK

The Scripture quotations contained herein are from the New Revised Standard Version Bible, copyright © 1989, by the Division of Christian Education of the National Council of the Churches of Christ in the U.S.A., are are used by permission. All rights reserved.

The rights of Bill Denning as author and illustrator of this work have been asserted in accordance with the Copyright, Designs and Patents Act 1988.

A CIP catalogue record for this book is available from the British Library.

Printed in Guernsey, Channel Islands

CONTENTS

Page

6. MAYPOLE FARM AND ITS CHAPEL
9. USING THIS BOOK
10. LETTING GO – A look at the theme

13. Meditation 1: LETTING GO OF THE SNARE Psalm 124 and Luke 5:17-26
23. Meditation 2: LETTING GO OF BARRIERS Psalm 122 and Luke 9:51-56
33. Meditation 3: LETTING GO OF FAILURE Psalm 147:1-11, 12-13, Luke 5:12-13
43. Meditation 4: LETTING GO OF THE FAMILIAR Psalm 107 and Matthew 8:18-22
53. Meditation 5: LETTING GO OF THE PAST Psalm 23 and Luke 24:28-32

62. CONCLUSION.

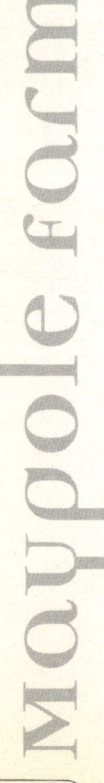

MAYPOLE FARM AND ITS CHAPEL

Maypole Farm has been around for well over two centuries and apart from changing its thatched roof for a tiled one, perhaps in the 19th century, it looks much the same as when it was built all those years ago in the heart of the South Gloucestershire countryside. There is one distinctive difference and that is the chapel, which was once a store for cider apples. With its whitewashed walls, candles and a window that looks out on grass and trees, the chapel has become holy ground for a number of people who treasure its simple beauty and share in its contemplative life. A growing collection of icons made from natural wooden shapes and textures is a more recent addition because creativity of all kinds is part of the life here. Poetry, stories and prayers are written, pictures are painted and clay is modelled and the evidence is all around.

The monthly Eucharist and regular Quiet Days and Retreats are where most of the meditations in this book were first used and are regularly made available to people who come to the farm for spiritual direction or as part of their life-long search for wholeness.

THE CHAPEL

For many years the chapel was a small, dimly lit and rather intimate place. It became familiar and was loved and valued as it was but the time came to think about letting in more light and making more space. It was not bad, wrong or inadequate as it was – but the time had come to let go of the past and to change quite radically. The secure, private little room that was opened up suddenly showed the grass and trees and in late winter the snowdrops followed by primroses. There was a new awareness of the movement of seasons with the trees losing their leaves and then growing them in spring. There was a new awareness of the weather – the sun, the wind and the rain. The birds – robins, blackbirds, thrushes, magpies – and above everything else the light, the ever changing light.

Before we started the changes there were fears as well as hopes. There could be a loss of intimacy and privacy alongside the anticipation of something more rich and beautiful. There were doubts and misgivings and a fear of the unknown. The familiar would be lost and there could be no going back. The chaos and mess when the wall was first opened up with endless dust and heaps of stone and rubble to be moved was alarming but the working party cleaned, filled and painted. Furnishings and fabrics were completed and the day came for the Opening – a perfect September day of sun and joy. Let the changes in the chapel be a model of what could happen for you in meditation.

Let light into your secret places. Dare to look with a new awareness at the world around. Dare to dream your hopes and allow your fears to be challenged and healed.

The chapel

The Chapel at Maypole Farm where cider apples were once stored.

The drawing shows where the large blocked up doorway at the end of the chapel was opened up to gain access up two steps into what was a woodshed. Carpet, hessian curtains and chairs replace firewood and icons hang on the walls. Everywhere there is light.

USING THIS BOOK

There is no expectation that you should begin with the first meditation and work your way through its suggestions to the end. Glance through what is there perhaps noting the practical resources on offer and then start with an issue that catches your imagination and stay with it for as long as you wish. That might be one day or it could be spread over a week giving you time to explore the questions in greater depth. Play with the material and let it touch you where it will. Each unit begins with a prayer and has a psalm and related gospel story. It includes questions and suggestions for getting into those texts and then a reflection built round the prayer. The meditation concludes with a poem and these too have a meditative quality, and almost all of them are abridged versions of something longer.

PRACTICAL RESOURCES At the end of each of the sections there are two pages of practical ideas; these are marked by a candle. They are of a general nature and are not specific to that particular unit. You might wish to look at some of these before beginning the meditations.
They include:

- Ways to get more deeply into meditation and being aware of the body with its senses.
- Thoughts about keeping a journal and finding a trusted friend with whom to share insights.
- Ways of using mantras, the senses and rituals and being in touch with yourself.

The drawings are not illustrations to the readings so much as a stimulus to the imagination. Let them interact with the written meditations or let them be something in their own right.

LETTING GO — A LOOK AT THE THEME

'Wimps and Wasps' happens to be a convenient image that surfaced in a conversation one day when we were exploring the way that some people cling on and others cut off as survival strategies. The wimp hangs on pathetically, possibly sulking and certainly snivelling. The wasp gets in with a sharp sting before disappearing with a hard-edged rejection. Both are ways of handling threatening situations and are intended to offer forms of protection from further pain and both are very largely driven by fear.

Those who habitually cling might fear rejection and hang on desperately to a lifestyle or relationship that could be profoundly destructive and yet there is a firm conviction that to stay in it is the only viable option. Those who cut off may well be trying to get in first with a hurtful rejection fearing that it will inevitably happen to them anyway. Their defence is to detach rapidly and to withdraw into what might appear to be safe isolation. Neither the wasp nor the wimp feels very comfortable about being so trapped on the edge of crisis always waiting for the next bad thing to happen. It is not safe and never brings the longed for security or happiness and yet it persists.

'Letting Go' looks at some of the questions we need to ask if we are to resolve some of the issues in the many relationships that make up our lives. This will not happen overnight. Indeed those ways may be around in some form or other for a lifetime but moving on has to begin somewhere. Once we understand that the discomfort to our foot is no more than a stone in our shoe, we immediately remove the offending object. Sadly our destructive patterns are not like stones in our shoes. These patterns are profoundly interwoven with our whole lives and cannot be removed painlessly.

The healing process is not about cutting something out and throwing it away. It would make it easier if that were so. It is about healing the way we react to all that happens. The change is fundamental. It is not about moving the furniture round or doing some re-decorating. It is much more about looking at the whole house from its foundations upwards, and putting right what is fundamentally wrong. That exercise can be painful and traumatic and it involves change and, of course, much letting go.

A house near where I live had a persistent crack working its way down from the top to the bottom and it suddenly got much worse. The solution was drastic. It involved the need to go right under the building in order to create a new concrete raft, which itself had concrete piles that went down to the bedrock. This was done slowly and methodically working all round the foundations of the house and taking great care that the whole building did not collapse in the process. That danger was always present.

No doubt the warning signs were there for years and presumably they patched up the cracks but always they would open and get worse. The parable for our own lives is clear enough. There comes a time when we cannot put it off any longer and we have to do something. When the family living there was faced by the prospect of so much upheaval I have no doubt they did everything they could to find an alternative that would not involve so drastic a solution. But in the end they faced it. And so must we.

Taking these meditations seriously and staying with the prayers and suggestions can offer a way of addressing and challenging some of the issues that have to be faced however unpalatable it may sometimes seem. Though it is a slow process change does happen. Learning how to let go may be costly and difficult – and yet when we do, we start to live.

Letting go

12

LETTING GO OF THE SNARE

PRAYER: 'O God who comes to us in love'

READINGS: Psalm 124 and Luke 5:17-26 'The Paralysed Man'

EXPLORATION of the psalm and the story

REFLECTIVE MEDITATION on the prayer.

POEM: 'Angels Wings'

RESOURCE: 'Getting into meditation and relaxation'

meditation one

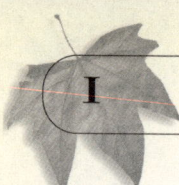

1 LETTING GO OF THE SNARE *Psalm 124 and Luke 5:17-26*

Meditation one

O God who comes to us in love
to rescue us from our enemies:
forgive us when we choose
to live dangerously near to hidden snares
and when our struggling feelings
threaten to drown us in their waves.
When we lie paralysed, weak and helpless
and cling to our disease

we give you thanks for those whose love
calls them to carry us with the arms of Christ
and whose care drives them
to bring us to the place
where sins are forgiven
ounds are healed and we let go
of threatening traps that hold us.
Through Jesus Christ we pray. Amen.

'The Paralysed Man Lets Go of the Snare'

Psalm 124 (NRSV) If it had not been God who was on our side – let Israel now say – if it had not been God who was on our side when our enemies attacked us, then they would have swallowed us up alive, when their anger was kindled against us then the flood would have swept us away, the torrent would have gone over us; then over us would have gone the raging waters. Blessed be God, who has not given us as prey to their teeth. We have escaped like a bird from the snare of the fowlers; the snare is broken, and we have escaped.

The Story. Luke 5:17-26 (NRSV) One day, while he was teaching, Pharisees and teachers of the law were sitting near by (they had come from every village of Galilee and Judea and from Jerusalem); and the power of the Lord was with him to heal. Just then some men came, carrying a paralysed man on a bed. They were trying to bring him in and lay him before Jesus; but finding no way to bring him in because of the crowd, they went up on the roof and let him down with his bed through the tiles into the middle of the crowd in front of Jesus. When he saw their faith, he said, 'Friend, your sins are forgiven you.' Then the scribes and the Pharisees began to question, 'Who is this who is speaking blasphemies? Who can forgive sins but God alone?' When Jesus perceived their questionings, he answered them, 'Why do you raise such questions in your hearts? Which is easier, to say, "Your sins are forgiven you," or to say, "Stand up and walk?" But so that you may know that the Son of Man has authority on earth to forgive sins [he said to the one who was paralysed] I say to you, stand up and take your bed and go to your home.' Immediately he stood up before them, took what he had been lying on, and went to his home, glorifying God. Amazement seized all of them, and they glorified God and were filled with awe, saying, 'We have seen strange things today.'

EXPLORING THE PSALM AND THE STORY

It may be helpful to take just one or two of the suggestions or questions at a time. Too many at once could be indigestible. Go for the ones that make you look twice.

The psalm uses some powerful imagery when it speaks of the way God is with us, and Luke's story has a range of equally powerful images with the sick man having to be carried by a perilous route to the feet of Jesus. In this meditation we have the opportunity to use those expressions of human experience and to do so by linking the psalm with the paralysed man.

- Make a note of the visual images in both the psalm and the story and put alongside that list some of the feelings you imagine might be present in them.

Let your imagination work with the images used in the psalm as they relate to the paralysed man:
- What kind of feelings might have 'swallowed him alive'?
- What might the 'raging waters' be that could have gone over his head, almost drowning him?
- What stops him letting go of these feelings?
- What might his 'snare' be that is broken when he is healed?
- Might there have been a part of him that would have clung to his illness?
- Jesus sent him home carrying the very thing he had been lying on. How do you imagine he felt when he let his paralysis go and did not need help?
- Read the psalm as if you were the man who can now walk again.

Now go on to explore how many of your responses to those questions reflect your own journey. Think about what paralyses you deep inside and what the waves might be that threaten to wash over your head until you feel you cannot go on. Ask yourself what might happen if you let go of that way of life.

STAY WITH YOURSELF AND LISTEN TO YOUR OWN NEED

- Who is 'on your side' and who carries you to a healing place?
- What does it feel like to be dependent on others?
- What might have to be broken through to get to the healing place?
- What might you have to leave behind and what might need forgiveness to make your healing possible?
- What might 'going home' mean for you? And how might you feel going home alone?

What have your snares or paralyses been?
Where have you experienced a snare being broken as the paralysis has left you and did you walk 'home' with freedom and joy?
Who has been there for you today? Give thanks and choose to receive their faithful liberating love.

PUT THE FOCUS NOW ON OTHER PEOPLE

- Who today may feel engulfed and alone and at the mercy of destructive forces, and who may feel trapped?
- A way of staying with their pain might be to think of them as paralysed. How might they feel?
- What is doing this to them, and who can faithfully carry them to the healing place where Christ is present?

Visualise them letting go the snare of their paralysis and returning home. Could you assist this process?

A REFLECTIVE MEDITATION ON THE PRAYER

O God who comes to us in love
to rescue us from our enemies:
*You know all about my enemies
in a way I can never know.
You see into the depths of me
struggling and clinging
and pitying myself
and all the time my hidden enemies
trap me and taunt me
and tell me I am bad.*

Forgive us when we choose
to live dangerously near to hidden snares
and when our struggling feelings
threaten to drown us in their waves.

*Forgive me and in your love
free me from my snares
and the waves of feeling
washing over me.*

*You are close by
but sometimes
often
I do not know that you are there
when anger tears my heart
and fears disturb my soul
and I lose touch with those I love
whose hands and words are Christ's.*

When we lie paralysed, weak and helpless
and cling to our dis-ease
we give you thanks for those whose love
calls them to carry us with the arms of Christ
and whose care
drives them to bring us to the place
where sins are forgiven
wounds are healed and we let go
of threatening traps that hold us.
   *I give you thanks and dare
   to leave my snares and walk again.*
Through Jesus Christ we pray. Amen

POEM: ANGELS WINGS

I felt the sound of angels wings
and heard a silent whisper
in the darkness of the night
and for a moment knew beyond all knowing
who I am when shaped
by pain and love
by love and pain.
Sorrow and joy and love
join gentle wounded hands
and banish fear
but cannot will not should not banish pain
when all that fear had grasped had been let go.

The deepest wounds that bleed
in quiet stillness
far beyond the edge of measured time
are held within the heart of One
whose name is Love
And here I dare to touch the mystery
of broken bread and wine
that waits and waits within eternity

and feels the emptying that asks
for nothing in return.
Then comes the unsought gift on angels' wings
the gift of peace that always waits
within the depths
to hear the call of love and reaches out
to meet and touch the grief
till all the tearing ugliness
of unacknowledged pain is whole and clean.

For pain alone can measure love's intensity
within the awesome silence of your love.

And in this place beyond the edge
of measured space and time
there is an ecstasy more near to tears
for here I know and I am known
and in that inner knowing
of my darkness and my light
I find the One
who never for one moment had lost me.

MEDITATION AND RELAXATION: *Some thoughts and ideas*

Time, space and stillness are essentials. In the art class that I run, I frequently remind others and myself that there is no absolutely right way to paint or draw. What we need to do is to find out the best way for each of us and to develop that way calling on as many resources and ideas as possible. There is always something new to learn and the journey is an exciting one. Meditation is the same.

In this meditation and indeed in all of them it is suggested that you spend time with some of the questions. That does not mean every question or even in the order that they are. To do this you need to give yourself time and space. Let us look at what might help you to get the most out of it if you are coming at it for the first time. In different ways you have probably meditated without giving it that name. Think for a moment about those occasions on holiday when you did not have to hurry or get things done and you had time to be still and space to let your senses take in what was there. You probably began to feel quite deeply too.

The heart of meditation is about being quiet in the presence of God, listening and being reflective, sensitive, thoughtful and aware. It can happen anywhere but the truth is that the place where you pray can help or get in the way of what you want to do.

- **QUIET SPACE** Ideally you need to have space where you can be comfortable and still where there will be no interruptions. Those with young families might find this almost impossible but it is worth struggling to get what you need and it may be necessary to declare what your boundaries are on this and ask firmly for co-operation.

RESOURCE: RELAXATION

Tension, stress and anxiety all make meditation more difficult, if not impossible. It is hard to focus on the bible readings and prayers with an open heart and mind when worries are pressing on the consciousness. Those worries cannot and should not be dismissed. They have to be addressed sooner or later. It might help if they are really getting in the way to acknowledge them almost formally, and note them down in your notebook or journal if you have one. You commit yourself to return to those issues that are clamouring for attention – but only after you have completed a substantial part of your meditation. You can return to the day's issues with a clearer mind and a deeper sense of the presence of Christ who shares those concerns with you.

- Breathing and body posture are supremely important. Whether sitting or lying, attend first to your breathing.

- Breathe in firmly and hold for a moment and let go. Go on doing this several times and return to it from time to time if disturbing and unwanted thoughts return.

- Some people use a simple phrase to go with the breathing in and the breathing out. The one I use most is: *'Jesus Christ in your love, forgive my sins, heal my wounds and set me free.'* You could try a shorter version or maybe even just *'Jesus Christ'*. Try breathing in on *'Jesus'* and out on *'Christ'* repeating this for as long as you want or need. It is prayer.

- Relax your body. Tension is often focused around the neck and shoulders, but the face, arms, legs and hands can all be too tense. One by one focus on these areas and tighten the relevant muscles and let them go. Return occasionally to your breathing and focus on what is happening to your breath.

Letting go

22

LETTING GO OF BARRIERS

PRAYER: 'O God who waits with love'

READINGS: Psalm 122 and Luke 9:51-56 'They did not receive him'

EXPLORATION of the psalm and the story

REFLECTIVE MEDITATION on the prayer

POEM: 'The Captive Butterfly'

RESOURCE: 'Keeping a Journal' and story writing

LETTING GO OF BARRIERS

Psalm 122 and Luke 9:51-56

O God who waits with love
until we are ready to be open to you:
give us the courage
to break down the walls
that keep us in darkness and ignorance,
and that separate us
from you and one another.

Open our eyes to catch your vision for us
and all humanity
and for the earth
and all its creatures
and give us the will and the grace
to live that dream with faithfulness and joy.
Through Jesus Christ we pray. Amen

Meditation Two

WALLS OF PEACE AND WALLS OF HATE

Psalm 122 (NRSV)
I was glad when they said to me, 'Let us go to the house of the Lord!'
Our feet are standing within your gates, O Jerusalem.
Jerusalem – built as a city that is bound firmly together.
To it the tribes go up, the tribes of the Lord, as was decreed for Israel, to give thanks to the name of the Lord.
For there the thrones for judgement were set up, the thrones of the house of David.
Pray for the peace of Jerusalem: 'May they prosper who love you.
Peace be within your walls, and security within your towers.'
For the sake of my relatives and friends I will say, 'Peace be within you.'
For the sake of the house of the Lord our God, I will seek your good.

Luke 9:51-56 (NRSV) When the days drew near for him to be taken up, he set his face to go to Jerusalem. And he sent messengers ahead of him. On their way they entered a village of the Samaritans to make ready for him; but they did not receive him, because his face was set toward Jerusalem.
When his disciples James and John saw it, they said, 'Lord, do you want us to command fire to come down from heaven and consume them?' But he turned and rebuked them.
Then they went on to another village.

EXPLORING THE PSALM AND THE STORY

We teach our little children never to trust a stranger, sadly and rightly so. It is one of the harsh boundaries that they learn. It is impossible to imagine a community or a relationship where there are no 'walls' of any kind. It is unrealistic to envisage the possibility even. In theory 'walls' exist to protect us from danger and we justify their existence in our worlds of work, worship, family and friendship.

But equally sadly we use them to protect us from taking courageous risks of trust in our relationships. The wall can be a safe and necessary boundary or a destructive barrier to love. Boundaries are essential in society but barriers built on prejudice are not. A boundary is an agreed limit on what is appropriate and what is not and is in place to protect. A barrier could be a wall that is put in place and may not be to protect but to divide. It is these dividing, destructive walls that separate us from God, one another, the earth and ourselves on which we focus in these mediations.

THE PSALM speaks of the true security within the walls that are there not to divide but to contain and protect and to give the true freedom of safety where there can be a deep and lasting peace.

THE STORY highlights the traditional enmity between two communities that could have been one and we see the disappointing sectarian response of the disciples that triggers the frustration of Jesus.

The exercise begins to explore some of these boundaries and barriers in ourselves, but they could equally be in the communities where we live, work and worship.

RECOLLECTION
- Think about your everyday world and assess where you experience barriers between you and other people. Reflect on where you sense barriers between yourself and God. And maybe you could think about dividing walls within yourself. Don't try to handle all these at once. Choose one to work with and perhaps come back another day to the others when you are ready.

FEELINGS
- The barriers already noted will have produced a range of emotions. Note the feelings now in order to be more willing to own them and to become more open to the kind of change that the long slow healing process will involve.

ANALYSIS
- Explore the history of these barriers; they did not appear by chance. Recall childhood experiences that caused those walls to be there and adult experiences that have reinforced their existence.

OUTCOME
- What practical effects does this have on your day-to-day life and work and upon your quiet space with God each day?

RESPONSE
- You want to move on? How realistically will you pray the prayer for today? Where will you look for a more open and trusting companionship on this next stage of your journey?

AND NOW? Take just one of those barriers you chose in the exercise and decide today what action you could take in order to begin to answer the prayer used in this meditation.

A REFLECTIVE MEDITATION ON THE PRAYER

O God who waits with love
until we are ready to be open to you:
We give you thanks that you wait
not in anger but in healing love.
Forgive us our unwillingness
to act with courage
but our fear is great.
We wait in hope and quiet trust.
Give us the courage to break down the walls
that keep us in darkness and ignorance,
and that separate us from you and one another.
  The walls are high because
  we have made them so
  to keep others from us
  in case they should see too much
  and reject us
  and they are thick to keep us
  safe from attack
  yet all they have done is kept us
  in the darkness of our ignorance.
  And in our futile desperation
  we have tried to hide from you
  and even from ourselves.
Open our eyes to catch your vision for us
and all humanity
and for the earth and all its creatures.
And give us the will and the grace
to live that dream with faithfulness and joy.
  You have called to us
  and you have dreamed your dream
  within us
  of a world at peace
  of a church at peace
  of women and men at peace.
  of the earth and all its creatures.
  Give us grace and give us faith
  and give us love
  so that the barriers may be destroyed
  and joy may be released
  and the freedom of the children of God
  may be theirs and ours now and for ever.
Through Jesus Christ we pray.   Amen.

POEM: THE CAPTIVE BUTTERFLY

Batter your fragile wings O little one
against unyielding glass
called on by summer golden light
and gentle warmth
called on by burning love
to leave the cold dark prison
where your soul
is frozen locked and safe
and where your heart
is winter chilled and held unmoved
where buried feelings lie
untouched unheard.

You wait the call to be
to float upon the wind
and drink pure honey
from a hundred glorious flowers
and taste the fierce sharp pain
of freedom's ecstasy -
and all the risk of heaven
and deepest hell.

Batter your growing wings
against unyielding glass
and wait the gentle hand that lifts the catch
itself so deeply scarred with nails and thorns
and you are free to fly with angels far
beyond the prison's grasp.

And far beyond that grasp the chalice waits
held by those same scarred hands
and you are free to drink
the sacred wine of heaven
and eat that bread he gives.

These brilliant shining wings
the choice – the awesome choice
the love that heals –
all these are yours.

Batter your wings against the barrier glass
let go and live.

RESOURCE: KEEPING A JOURNAL

Quite frequently the questions used in this book invite a written response and when it comes to handling stirred up feelings, writing can be enormously liberating. The journal can be a place to record what is happening to you and it gives an opportunity to reflect privately by encouraging feelings to be expressed. Journals need be no more than a simple notebook where perhaps thoughts, feelings and some significant events are recorded. But it could be much more than that and could warrant a hard backed plain book that feels more significant and serious. Some people use their PCs for this – I do.

THOUGHTS AND FEELINGS As you reflect on some of the questions raised by the meditations you might care to note your responses. One of the most important will be your feelings. Never ignore what your heart is saying to you through your emotions. We are concerned not only with the heart but also the mind. That could mean listing some of the challenging questions that begin to surface. Do not look too hard for answers. Go first for the questions raised for you.

POETRY AND PRAYERS You may well wish to write some poetry or prayers. Do them your way and believe in your way. With poetry you might like to use rhyme but do not be bound by it. Let your words flow with a rhythm and use as many visual images as you can and pile up those words that express emotion. Writing your prayers too can simply be an outpouring from your heart. The psalms are often exactly that. It can help to get things happening, to imagine you are the person in the story and to express the prayer or longing that you imagine to be there. No one need see what you write so you need not fear being judged.

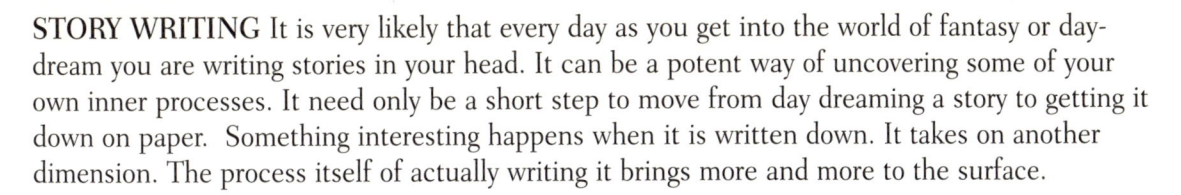

STORY WRITING It is very likely that every day as you get into the world of fantasy or daydream you are writing stories in your head. It can be a potent way of uncovering some of your own inner processes. It need only be a short step to move from day dreaming a story to getting it down on paper. Something interesting happens when it is written down. It takes on another dimension. The process itself of actually writing it brings more and more to the surface.

TAKING THE STORY FURTHER Another direction for writing is to let your imagination get to work on what might happen afterwards to the characters in the meditation story. The stories that we have in the gospels are usually short and to the point and often we know nothing more about the people involved and what happened to them. At one of the Creative Eucharists at Maypole Farm where we were looking at the story of Mary Magdalene in the Resurrection garden, a number of people wrote the narrative from her perspective. They let Mary tell it from her point of view. It opened many doors for the writers and for us all.

SHARING YOUR JOURNAL While you might not wish to hand that precious document over to anyone else, you might well want to take up some issues that have surfaced with that person you really can trust. It is worth noting those issues as you go along and then raising them at an appropriate time. On many questions two minds are better than one.

A journal is essentially something very private and personal and, to state the obvious, it should not be left around for anyone to read. Finally, don't let this kind of writing be a burden or duty. Just do it when you feel like doing it. But be warned, the habit can become compulsive!

Letting go

32

LETTING GO OF FAILURE

PRAYER: 'O God whose boundless love is offered to all'

READINGS: Psalm 147:1-11 and 12-13 Luke 5:12-13 The Leper

EXPLORATION of the psalm and the story

REFLECTIVE MEDITATION on the prayer

POEM: 'You lie hidden in the depths'

RESOURCE: 'The Senses' Praying with more than words

3 LETTING GO OF FAILURE

Psalm 147:1-11 and 12-13 Luke 5:12-13

O God whose boundless love
is offered to all:
forgive us for the wounding
we have done to others
and the hurt we have done
to ourselves.

Bind our aching wounds
that need your care
and as renewing rain falls softly in the dark
on dry and thirsty hills
so let your healing love
fall gently on us as we wait.
Through Jesus Christ we pray.   Amen.

'THE LEPER'

Psalm 147 (NRSV)
Praise the Lord! How good it is to sing praises to our God; for he is gracious, and a song of praise is fitting.
The Lord builds up Jerusalem; he gathers the outcasts of Israel.
He heals the broken-hearted, and binds up their wounds.
He determines the number of the stars; he gives to all of them their names.
Great is our Lord, and abundant in power; his understanding is beyond measure.
The Lord lifts up the downtrodden; he casts the wicked to the ground.
Sing to the Lord with thanksgiving; make melody to our God on the lyre.
He covers the heavens with clouds, prepares rain for the earth, makes grass grow on the hills.
He gives to the animals their food, and to the young ravens when they cry.
His delight is not in the strength of the horse, nor his pleasure in the speed of a runner;
but the Lord takes pleasure in those who fear him, in those who hope in his steadfast love.

Luke 5:12-13 (NRSV) Once, when he was in one of the cities, there was a man covered with leprosy. When he saw Jesus, he bowed with his face to the ground and begged him, 'Lord, if you choose, you can make me clean.'
Then Jesus stretched out his hand, touched him, and said, 'I do choose. Be made clean.' Immediately the leprosy left him.

EXPLORING THE PSALM AND THE STORY

In today's prayer we focus on the highly charged issue of forgiveness and the healing that can follow. If you are going to go more deeply into it through meditation, set yourself the goal of not having a guilt trip either about your own failures that need forgiving or the forgiving of those who have wronged you. Excessive guilt is dangerous and unhealthy where it is easy to be sucked down into a dark place of feeling quite unforgivable.

The opposite of having no sense of wrong at all is perhaps equally unhealthy. In this meditation attempt to achieve a balanced approach. It can be done.

'GETTING IT WRONG'

- **RECOLLECTION** Recall a situation where you did something you now believe to be wrong. Do not give yourself a hard time but try to be honest.
- **FEELINGS** How did you feel at the time? And what do you feel now as you remember?
- **ANALYSIS** Analyse it gently by reflecting on what happened and why. It may help to do this by asking whether you chose it or whether it was more like a mistake or an error. Was anyone else involved?
- **OUTCOME** What happened as a result of your action? Is there anything around in the present that still relates to it?
- **RESPONSE** In the light of this reflection what action do you now feel you need or would like to take in the present? Who or what may help you to do this?

'FORGIVING YOURSELF'

You need not remain in the bad place that this delicate issue often represents. It is important to deal with what needs to be forgiven so that you can then let it go and move on. In the story the leper would almost certainly have believed that his illness was a direct result of his sin and he would have been an outcast. In its crude form this is obviously not a view we hold today but often there is a link between our unhealed failures and our physical and emotional health.

- Reflect on the possible links between your physical and your emotional health

The prayer refers to our need to forgive ourselves.
Is this difficult for you? It is sometimes said that it is easier to forgive others than to forgive ourselves.

- Reflect on what you feel towards yourself because of your failure
- Go on to remind yourself that God loves you as you are and not as you hope to become

The Psalm in its poetry reminds us that God 'heals the broken-hearted and binds up their wounds'. You may feel quite broken-hearted about your failure and deeply wounded because of it. As you go into the final meditation based on the prayer, do so with a deep trust in the healing love of God who longs to make you whole.

There is an image in the psalm of healing: the renewing rain that makes grass grow on the parched and dry hills and this is picked up in the prayer. Visualise the barren wastes being refreshed by rain.

A REFLECTIVE MEDITATION ON THE PRAYER

O God whose boundless love
is offered to all:
*hear our prayer when the night is dark
and the sense of failure lies deep within us.
Help us to know that we all receive
from your generous heart,
and as you welcomed the leper
so no one is turned from you.*
O God whose boundless love is offered to all:
forgive us for the wounding
we have done to others
and the hurt we have done to ourselves.
*You understand all that drives us
into places that hurt and destroy
both ourselves and one another.*

*Help us to know that our chosen wrong
and the failure of others
is often inter-woven
with our deep and desperate need
to be valued and loved.*

*Show us today that we are loved
and that it is possible
to love and value ourselves
without destructive self-absorption.*
Bind our aching wounds that need your care
And as renewing rain falls softly in the dark
on dry and thirsty hills:
so let your healing love fall on us as we wait.
*Bind our aching wounds
with all your healing grace
and show us how to know
as one poor leper knew
that in your love you choose
to make us clean.
Let gentle healing love
fall softly on us as we wait
for you alone can make us whole.
Let healing love fall gently on us now.*

Through Jesus Christ we pray.

POEM: 'YOU LIE HIDDEN IN THE DEPTHS'

God my maker you lie hidden in the depths
almost beyond imagination's reach
and far beyond our sense or thought.
Feeling alone can touch the mystery
as awe and wonder fear and dread
delight and joy join hands
and take me to the place where no paths lie
and none have ever been before.

And here within these forest depths
where I must walk alone I meet the One
whose hands whose face are scarred
whose burning eyes shall see beyond
the masks I wear to hide my fear
whose listening ears shall hear beyond
the half true lies I use to win control
whose gentle voice shall speak
with quiet strength to draw me close
whose touch shall heal the hidden wounds
who comes with flaming love
to make me whole.

Letting go of failure

RESOURCE: THE SENSES

Touch, taste, smell, seeing and hearing. We are sensual people and so we should be. It is through those senses that we interact with the world around us. The loss of any one of those gifts is a serious deprivation. In drama workshops I have sometimes used an exercise where participants have worked in pairs where one is blindfold. One immediate consequence is the heightening of the other senses. As people feel their way around not daring to trust their partner, touch is paramount. But once confidence is gained there is an exploration of the immediate environment that can be profoundly moving. It is fascinating to watch a young child gently leading an elderly person with great care and attentiveness and offering them a flower to smell or a surface to feel. So where might our senses relate to prayer?

EYES CLOSED! My childhood experiences of prayer seemed always to include one basic element – eyes must be closed! The mere mention of it takes me straight back to school! I also recall being told when we first went to Bristol and lived not far from Muller's Homes, that the huge barrack-like buildings to house the children had high windows in them so that children would not look out and see the wicked world. It would appear that their inherent badness must not be encouraged by seeing too much!

CANDLES Most of us like candles. I have more than once been accused of candle worship – a charge I can happily live with. There is something about the gentle silence of the flame that touches a chord. Candles can be very beautiful. We use them a lot in our chapel at Maypole Farm.

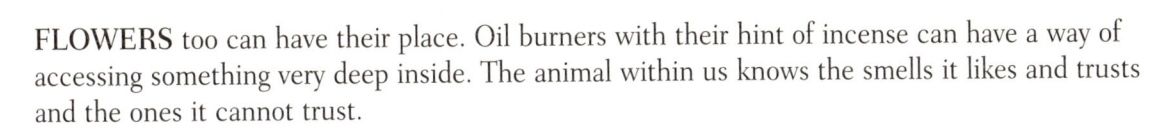

FLOWERS too can have their place. Oil burners with their hint of incense can have a way of accessing something very deep inside. The animal within us knows the smells it likes and trusts and the ones it cannot trust.

ICONS and CROSSES These have a focusing quality and are usually quite specific and can draw the eye beyond what is seen to what is unseen.

MUSIC? Or is it total silence that you need? Needs vary and the options are endless. In another meditation there are some thoughts about relaxation and the body, but it would naturally belong here simply to refer to whether you want to sit, lie on the floor or kneel. Or you might well choose to go out walking. Experiment and find what is right for you.

IMAGES and FEELING In this meditation that looks at failure and forgiveness, we might care to develop some of the suggestions here that involve the senses. It would be perfectly possible to look for and find images that express the brokenness that failure is. You could contemplate that image for a few minutes and let it speak. We are good at seeing failure. Are we so able to look for and find images of healing and forgiveness? Hymns are full of forgiveness and healing. You might choose to find and sing to yourself one that touches you deeply and says what your words find it hard to say.

You may have a favourite piece of music or a poem that does the same thing. Recalling times when you have forgiven another and have been forgiven yourself could touch you deeply. If you could link those experiences with something that you touch, hear or see, there can be a significant affirmation.

Letting Go

WCD 83

Blaina April 17. 83

42

LETTING GO OF THE FAMILIAR

PRAYER: 'Stay with us Lord Jesus Christ when we must cross over to the other side'

READINGS: Psalm 107 and Matthew 8:18-22 Let go and 'Follow me'

EXPLORATION of the psalm and the story

REFLECTIVE MEDITATION on the prayer

POEM: THE DRAGONFLY 'Tremble your glistening wings'

RESOURCE: 'Trusted Friend' and 'Transition'

4 LETTING GO OF THE FAMILIAR *Psalm 107 and Matthew 8:18-22*

Stay with us Lord Jesus Christ
when we must cross over
to the other side
and move from where we are
to where we can be by your grace.
Forgive us when on that journey
we are overwhelmed by fears
and cannot sense
your saving presence with us
in those who touch us with your love.

Stir up in our hearts the faith
that challenges those fears
and enable us to respond
with awe and wonder
to the love that is for ever nearer
than our doubt.
In your name we pray.
Amen.

TOUGH CHOICES

Psalm 107 (NRSV)
O give thanks to the Lord, for he is good;
 for his steadfast love endures forever.
Let the redeemed of the Lord say so, those he redeemed from trouble
and gathered in from the lands, from the east and from the west,
from the north and from the south.
Some wandered in desert wastes, finding no way to an inhabited town;
hungry and thirsty, their soul fainted within them.
Then they cried to the Lord in their trouble,
and he delivered them from their distress;
he led them by a straight way, until they reached an inhabited town.
Let them thank the Lord for his steadfast love,
for his wonderful works to humankind.
For he satisfies the thirsty,
and the hungry he fills with good things.

Matthew 8:18-23 (NRSV) Now when Jesus saw great crowds around him, he gave orders to go over to the other side. A scribe then approached and said, 'Teacher, I will follow you wherever you go.' And Jesus said to him, 'Foxes have holes, and birds of the air have nests; but the Son of Man has nowhere to lay his head. Another of his disciples said to him, 'Lord, first let me go and bury my father.' But Jesus said to him, 'Follow me, and let the dead bury their own dead.' And when he got into the boat, his disciples followed him.

EXPLORING THE PSALM AND THE STORY

A few days before a Retreat at Maypole Farm, where we were using this story and the psalm with a focus on the words 'Jesus gave orders to cross over to the other side', I happened to see a dragonfly struggling out of the slime in our pond. Our cat shared my curiosity and made a lunge for the insect. In my attempt to protect it the cat was knocked sideways towards the pond and somehow managed to walk on water – or on water lilies to be more precise!

The dragonfly was engaged in a traumatic crossing over from the familiar place to the unknown and the journey was dangerous. In the psalm the poet speaks of the struggle to move on with time spent wandering in desert wastes, and experiencing hunger and thirst. Jesus calls his followers to 'cross over to the other side' and to continue with the next stage of the journey and there seems not to be much consultation about it. It would mean accepting some hardship and stress that might be involved but more than that it would mean change and becoming more real. We might well ask why is change with its loss of the familiar sometimes so threatening?

The psalm carries the message: *'Some wandered in desert wastes, finding no way to an inhabited town; hungry and thirsty, their soul fainted within them.'* It is not always so – it can be stirring, challenging and exciting. The psalm again: *'Let them thank the Lord for his steadfast love, for his wonderful works to humankind. For he satisfies the thirsty and the hungry he fills with good things.'* Let us explore both these aspects of the challenge.

- Recall a time as a child when you were pushed into 'crossing over' to another way of being. It might have been moving house against your will, or it could have been some inner struggle over a break up in the family. It was perhaps growing up itself. We are often not consulted as children. Children, it is sometimes said, are very resilient! Maybe

meditation four

the deeper truth is that children often hide what they feel when the well known world is shattered.

- How did you react to this? Were you alone in the experience or did it involve others?
- As you look back on that time, do you wish that you had handled it any other way or that there had been someone there for you?

If those questions were looking at being pushed into something against your will, recall now about a time where you chose to 'cross over' into something new. That might be about relationships or work.

- What feelings were stirred up in you by this?
- Who was around who really understood or was there no one to share the experience with you?
- As you reflect on this, what do you now feel that you needed most at that time?

The psalm: *'Then they cried to the LORD in their trouble, and he delivered them from their distress; he led them by a straight way, until they reached an inhabited town.'* Expressed in that way it sounds simple. The reality may well seem not quite so obvious. 'Crying to the Lord' in your trouble or joy for most of us involves another person who hears that cry.

- Who hears you without judgement, criticism or ridicule?
- As you look back can you see where a 'straight way' opened up before you as you 'crossed over'?
- The 'inhabited town' is about community. It is safe company and security. Where do you find that and in what ways can you be a safe haven for others?

A REFLECTIVE MEDITATION ON THE PRAYER

Stay with us Lord Jesus Christ
when we must cross over to the other side
and move from where we are
to where we can be by your grace.
> *You know that I prefer the comfort*
> *of what is familiar*
> *and where there is no change.*
> *I want to move*
> *and do not want to move.*
> *I want to change*
> *but fear is never far away.*

Forgive us when on that journey
we are overwhelmed by fears
> *I will go on that journey*
> *that calls me to grow up*
> *to become who I am –*
> *but the fears do overwhelm:*
> *fear of failure*
> *of ridicule*
> *of loneliness and despair.*
> *Forgive me in your love*
> *for this is how I am…*

and cannot sense
your saving presence with us
in those who touch us with your love.
> *Sometimes I do sense you*
> *in those who care*
> *and understand -*
> *in those who love*
> *when I am not loveable.*
> *And sometimes*
> *I do not know.*

Stir up in our hearts the faith
that challenges those fears
and enable us to respond
with awe and wonder
to that love that is for ever nearer
than our doubt.
In your name we pray. Amen.

POEM: THE DRAGONFLY TREMBLE YOUR GLISTENING WINGS

Tremble your glistening wings
break free from predators and slime
that cling
unfeeling of your need
imprisoning and dark.

Tremble your glistening wings
and let the sun's bright warmth
bring freedom from the world
you knew
and have outgrown.
Dangers wait
and yet more urgent than the fear
must be the longing to be free.
My caring hands will help you
and my watchful eyes will guard you
until the time shall come
to let you go.

And we shall meet in freedom
as you find your wings to bear you
high into the sky you had not known
that called you from your prison
that was home.

Tremble your glistening wings
called on by love
that sets you free

Letting go of the familiar

49

RESOURCE: A TRUSTED FRIEND

It may seem a contradiction to have a study on letting go of what is familiar and have a resource suggested that focuses on working with a trusted friend. It is quite deliberate. We are not meant to live in isolation. We need one another and that is a healthy and appropriate need to meet. The problem sometimes is about getting the balance right. We can lean too much or not enough. This person to whom you can really open your heart may or may not be a professional, but do if at all possible secure someone with whom you share your reflections on the stories and the questions that they raise. This is important. If you do not already do this I suspect that once you begin you will wonder why you never did it before. It might help to draw up a list of the qualities that you would want in this person. In workshops where this issue has arisen qualities often suggested have been 'confidentiality' and 'trust' and someone who will 'not judge or laugh at me'. It may be hard to find the ideal person and you might have to settle for something less, but try it.

CONTRACT You may already have experience of this kind of relationship through counselling or spiritual direction or you might well have a close friend with whom you share most things. If you can find the right one for you, that person will be of immeasurable worth. Some people work out a pattern where each listens to the other. If you go for this, it does require some discipline and perhaps a simple contract that each will have say half an hour or whatever is agreed. How often might you want to meet? If you are working through the meditations in a systematic way then it would be good to have a session once a week for a few weeks until you have completed it. If you are using the meditations in a less structured way, then presumably you would negotiate to meet when you needed it.

RESOURCE: TRANSITION

The meditation about 'crossing over' involves transition and much of life is precisely that. Just when we feel we have got a hold on things, the goal posts are moved and the familiar world melts away. This experience is a powerful resource if we see it that way and can use it with appropriate accompaniment.

LEAVING THE PLATEAU Some years ago I came to a place in my life that was very comfortable and secure. Looking back I call it my plateau. It proved to be a breathing space for the next stage of my journey in which I had to look long and hard at so much in myself where I needed to move on. The process was good but painful and it continues. The plateau was very comfortable, but it was not where I could stay. There was healing to be done and it took me right back to my childhood, revisiting places in my memory that I appeared to know very little about. Once the journey had begun I was carried along by it and I learned so much that was a liberation though a very painful one. I did not and I could not do this alone.

THE SECRETS OF YOUR HEART You might care to think of entering into these meditations as a process of attending to some of the closed off places in your story. You may well have put off doing this for a long time. You might feel willing to 'cross over to the other side' of your forgotten world. You might be unsettled and disturbed by taking some of the suggested questions seriously. Meditation is not always a recipe for comfort and indeed it can be the reverse in the short term. If however you have set about negotiating the wise provision of a good friend who is willing to share the secrets of your heart then you can move on and not look back.

Letting go of the familiar

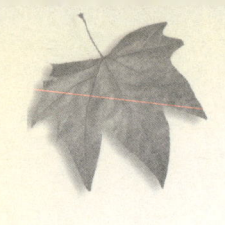

Letting go

LETTING GO OF THE PAST

PRAYER: 'Stay with us Lord Jesus Christ in the painful darkness'

READINGS: Psalm 23 and Luke 24:28-32 'Then their eyes were opened'

EXPLORATION of the psalm and the story.

REFLECTIVE MEDITATION on the prayer

POEM: 'Early we came'

RESOURCE: 'Ritual' 'Letting go' rituals, letter writing and prayers

5 — LETTING GO OF THE PAST

Psalm 23 and Luke 24:28-32

meditation five

Stay with us Lord Jesus Christ
in the painful darkness
of the chill and shadowed places
of our souls' long journey home.
Keep us mindful
of your Cross and Resurrection
that now and always
we may be sustained by truth and hope.
In your Name we pray. Amen.

THE HIDDEN STRANGER

Psalm 23 (NRSV)
The Lord is my shepherd, I shall not want.
He makes me lie down in green pastures; he leads me beside still waters; he restores my soul. He leads me in right paths for his name's sake.
Even though I walk through the darkest valley, I fear no evil; for you are with me; your rod and your staff – they comfort me.
You prepare a table before me in the presence of my enemies; you anoint my head with oil; my cup overflows.
Surely goodness and mercy shall follow me all the days of my life, and I shall dwell in the house of the Lord my whole life long.

Luke 24:28-32 (NRSV) As they came near the village to which they were going, he walked ahead as if he were going on. But they urged him strongly, saying, 'Stay with us, because it is almost evening and the day is now nearly over.' So he went in to stay with them. When he was at the table with them, he took bread, blessed and broke it, and gave it to them. Then their eyes were opened, and they recognised him; and he vanished from their sight. They said to each other, 'Were not our hearts burning within us while he was talking to us on the road, while he was opening the scriptures to us?'

LETTING GO OF THE PAST

It is a delicate business. There is a sense in which we inescapably carry the past and its traditions with us and not just in our memory. The suggestion of letting it go could seem insensitive or even foolish. There is however a huge difference between denying the past and letting go of it and it is all to do with how we relate to what has gone before. The two people on the road to Emmaus had to let go of the Jesus they knew and receive from the Christ who walked unknown and unrecognised beside them.

They had to leave behind an unrealisable dream of power and of liberation from Rome and catch a new vision. The past was full of powerful and relevant stories that they would remember and retell but they could not live in the past where those stories were first told. They could have clung to days gone by in a nostalgic and romantic way or in their bitterness they could have stamped on it and pretended that it had never meant anything. Learning how to relate to what has gone before neither hanging on to it nor denying it is utterly important.

LOSS In this exercise, have in mind groups or communities of which you are a part that have experienced loss.
- Have any dreams of your church or your community been lost, destroyed or squashed?
- What caused that to happen?
- Have any dreams of your family or close relationships been lost or destroyed? How?

Reflect on the emotions that were around at the time. Have you and they been able to come to terms with that loss and been able to let go of the feelings, or are they still around?

'STAY WITH US LORD JESUS CHRIST'

In today's prayer we acknowledge that life does sometimes bring some very painful experiences as that last exercise may have recalled. It may or may not be directly our own fault, but we have to choose how to handle these times when they happen. The psalm makes a brave affirmation of faith that dares to believe in the presence of God in the dark place. Luke's story has two people who are grieving a bitter disappointment and deep loss and they ask the mysterious stranger to stay with them.

Recall an occasion when you have felt betrayed or let down or when some bitter disappointment has threatened to change the whole course of your life and you have had to walk through a 'dark valley'.

- What did you feel at the time? Were you alone or were others involved with you as in the story?

Jesus the hidden stranger drew alongside.

- Who shared that experience with you in such a way that your whole attitude to the past and the future was changed?

They asked Jesus to stay with them.

- Who makes the presence of Jesus real for you today so that he 'stays with you' as you work out how to let go of the past?
- What makes your heart 'burn within you' or what helps it do that, as you let go of the past and catch a new vision for the future?

A REFLECTIVE MEDITATION ON THE PRAYER.

Stay with us Lord Jesus Christ
*Stay with us for you alone can meet
the aching needs of our hearts
and feed the unmet hunger
of our waiting souls.*

Stay with us in the painful darkness
of the chill and shadowed places
of our souls' long journey home.
*Stay with us we pray
when we must travel
through the bleak valley
where darkness is all around us
and we seem to be far from home.*

We dare to affirm
that we shall fear no evil
when you are beside us
and we shall be strong
with your love within us
a love that we know through those
*in whom we see your face
and from whose hands
we take the bread of life.*

Stay with us and keep us mindful
of your Cross and Resurrection
that now and always
we may be sustained by truth and hope.
*Stay with us and open to us
the mystery of your love
that our hearts may burn with wonder
as we glimpse the awesome truth
that life is sorrow and joy,
darkness and light
cross and resurrection
for with you beside us
your hope amongst us
and your truth within us
we shall not want in the hour of need.*

In your Name we pray. Amen

POEM: EARLY WE CAME — *The Women at the Tomb*

Early we came through moist deep
   shadows
   of the waiting dawn
our steps slow and senses numb
and then we heard
from far beyond the edge of space and time
a gentle sound of angels' wings

We stopped and in a timeless moment
senses stirred
and hearts now burned like fire
our souls awake

And from that distant edge
we heard the angels sing a Gloria
more glorious than all the golden light
of this new dawn
we had not seen for grief

And more mysterious still
the fierce strong rising sun shone deep
into the darkness of the tomb
now bright with dazzling light
that echoed in our hearts the angel song:
'He is not here.'

RESOURCE: RITUAL

Rituals like mantras are part of the unthinking routine of everyday life. We are doing things and using phrases all the time in a stylised way that signify something. Greetings and farewells are a good example. They vary widely in different cultures and we know where we are with our own traditions.

The Road to Emmaus story is full of rituals. Some belong to the world of courtesy as when Jesus made as if to go further, and he is invited to stay for a meal. The most striking ritual in the story is where Jesus takes the bread, blesses it, breaks it and gives it to the two.

'LETTING GO' RITUALS can have a great power to carry away some of the emotion that we need to lose. In this final meditation you might care to prepare some rituals that can take you a bit further along your journey. While you could do this alone, you could consider involving that trusted friend. Do prepare yourself before these things and make the most of them. They are not to be done casually. Do them with energy and commitment and prepare a prayer or mantra for before and after it. Here are some ideas:

- By the sea or river, name a rock or stone with something you wish to lose and throw it away.
- Take a leaf, decide what it represents or carries, and then drop it into a stream and watch it being carried away. Again, use a mantra or prayer to maximise your involvement.
- Blowing a dandelion head is another option, in season. Name what each blow represents.
- Writing a letter and burning it or tearing it up and throwing it in the bin is a well used resource.

LETTER WRITING can be extraordinarily effective. The letter could be to a person, to an institution or an organisation, to a family, to a group, to yourself even. At a Quiet Day recently someone wrote a letter to God. Be honest and direct and no one need see it though you might wish to share its contents with another.

With any of these rituals, consider having a form of words drawn perhaps from one of the readings or prayers to say as you do it. Use one that has come to mean something special for you. Another possibility would be something like: 'Jesus Christ in your love hear my prayer' for that ritual act is indeed a prayer.

- Commit yourself to doing something significant like going to a certain place that has a meaning for you. That is what a pilgrimage can be.
- You could ask for a special Eucharist or service or for prayers. 'Doing something' can carry considerable emotion when it involves others who really do understand and care.

POEMS AND PRAYERS Consider writing your own prayers, poems and mantras as a regular commitment to go alongside your meditation. You could prepare mantras from the texts you have been using to use with your times of relaxation. A healthy mantra repeated often enough is a powerful healing resource. Sadly, many of the mantras we use without thought are most damaging: for instance 'I never finish anything…' or 'I have nothing to say…' Saying the destructive thing often enough ensures that we really do believe it. The opposite is even more true. As we live with realistic affirmations that are drawn from the rich wells of our traditions and use them deliberately and with care, our lives are slowly transformed, very slowly.

CONCLUSION

Let us return to the house that had to have its foundations completely renewed. Perhaps as you have stayed with these meditations, you have looked at the foundations of your life and have recognised even more clearly that some of the weaknesses could no longer be handled by patching up but needed some hard work. So what next?

Perhaps you want to put right some of the failures that surrounded your childhood, but sometimes it threatens to get worse before it gets better. Change can be risky. The 'healing' of the house involved handing it over to others who had the skills and resources to do this. For most of us, handing our lives over to God includes trusting other people whose hearts beat with the love of Christ. To admit your need to one you trust is to open the door to the future. At the point when you recognise that you must do something with your life and you choose to involve others you 'let go'. This is not giving up responsibility for your life. It is about taking responsibility and revealing new possibilities where you are more open to God and more able to receive the healing care of others who work with you, not as an object to be mended but as a person to be known and loved.

Through meditation Christ is at work in you and is increasingly able to rebuild the foundations and repair the cracks. You will know that you are changing and it could be exciting or scary but today you can make a choice to keep faithful to this different way of being you. Decide what you have found to be most challenging and affirming as you have lived with these meditations and stay with that awareness. It may not mean a dramatic and immediate alteration but it could change the direction of the rest of your life as you move towards your future with confidence and hope. So join the butterfly: 'Batter your fragile wings – let go and live.'

A REFLECTIVE EXERCISE:
- Was there a meditation that touched you deeply and made you see yourself more clearly?
- What small step might you take today that responds to any insights and moves you forward?
- What help has the suggestion of a journal been to note your insights and responses and would you consider going on with it?
- If you were able to find a good and trusted friend with whom to share your reflection, what did you find most helpful about that experience? Have you told that person what you valued?

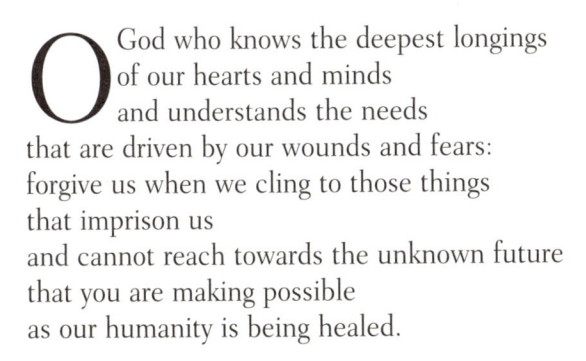

O God who knows the deepest longings
of our hearts and minds
and understands the needs
that are driven by our wounds and fears:
forgive us when we cling to those things
that imprison us
and cannot reach towards the unknown future
that you are making possible
as our humanity is being healed.

Challenge us by your Spirit
to review all our commitments
and to examine all our relationships
so that we may abandon everything
that destroys us
and may hold on with faith
to all that makes us whole.
Through Jesus Christ we pray.
Amen.

Letting Go